THE LIFE AND TIMES OF FANNY HILL

Adapted for the stage by April de Angelis

from the novel by John Cleland

samuelfrench.co.uk

For Amateur Production Enquiries

United Kingdom and World
excluding north america
plays@samuelfrench.co.uk
020 7255 4302/01

Each title is subject to availability from Samuel French,
depending upon country of performance.

THINKING ABOUT PERFORMING A SHOW?

There are thousands of plays and musicals available to perform from Samuel French right now, and applying for a licence is easier and more affordable than you might think

From classic plays to brand new musicals, from monologues to epic dramas, there are shows for everyone.

Plays and musicals are protected by copyright law so if you want to perform them, the first thing you'll need is a licence. This simple process helps support the playwright by ensuring they get paid for their work, and means that you'll have the documents you need to stage the show in public.

Not all our shows are available to perform all the time, so it's important to check and apply for a licence before you start rehearsals or commit to doing the show.

LEARN MORE & FIND THOUSANDS OF SHOWS

Browse our full range of plays and musicals and find out more about how to license a show
www.samuelfrench.co.uk/perform

Talk to the friendly experts in our Licensing team for advice on choosing a show, and help with licensing
plays@samuelfrench.co.uk   020 7387 9373

Acting Editions

BORN TO PERFORM

Playscripts designed from the ground up to work the way you do in rehearsal, performance and study

---

Larger, clearer text for easier reading

Wider margins for notes

Performance features such as character and props lists, sound and lighting cues, and more

---

+ CHOOSE A SIZE AND STYLE TO SUIT YOU

  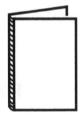

STANDARD EDITION

Our regular paperback book at our regular size

SPIRAL-BOUND EDITION

The same size as the Standard Edition, but with a sturdy, easy-to-fold, easy-to-hold spiral-bound spine

LARGE EDITION

A4 size and spiral bound, with larger text and a blank page for notes opposite every page of text. Perfect for technical and directing use

---

LEARN MORE | **samuelfrench.co.uk/actingeditions**

ABOUT THE AUTHOR

April De Angelis is an acclaimed writer whose extensive theatre work includes *My Brilliant Friend*, a two-part dramatisation of Elena Ferrante's epic family saga (Rose Theatre Kingston); *After Electra* (Theatre Royal Plymouth and Tricycle Theatre 2015); *Rune* (New Vic Theatre Stoke 2015); *Gastronauts* (Royal Court Upstairs, 2013); *Jumpy* (Royal Court 2011 and Duke of York's Theatre 2012, Melbourne and Sydney 2015); an adaptation of *Wuthering Heights* (Birmingham Rep, 2008); *A Laughing Matter* (Out of Joint at National Theatre, 2001); *A Warwickshire Testimony* (RSC, 1999); *The Positive Hour* (Out of Joint at Hampstead Theatre, 1997); *Playhouse Creatures* (revived at Chichester Festival Theatre in 2013); and *The Life And Times of Fanny Hill* (revived at the Bristol Old Vic, 2015).

April has also written the libretto for *Flight* music by Jonathan Dove, for Glyndebourne Opera; *The Silent Twins* libretto, which was set to music by Errollyn Wallen, Almeida Theatre, 2007; and *The Day After* at the ENO, 2017.

April's work for radio includes an adaptation of *Life In The Tomb* for BBC Radio 3 in 2014, a serialisation of *Peyton Place*, *Visitants* for BBC Radio 4, and *The Outlander* for Radio 5, which won the Writer's Guild Award in 1992.

TV work includes a BFI / Channel 4 commission, *Aristophanes*.

Photo credit: Johan Persson

MUSIC USE NOTE

All the songs in this play are readily available in the public domain.

The play was commissioned and first performed by the Red Shift Theatre Company at the Battersea Art Centre, directed by Jonathan Holloway in 1990.

CHARACTERS

VOLTAIRE
FANNY HILL
SPARK
LOUISA
SWALOW
FIDDLE
MOTHER BROWN
PHOEBE
DINGLE
MR CROFTS
MRS JONES
MAID
SERVANT BOY
MR H
MRS COLE
MR NORBERT
NOSEGAY SELLER

Part One

A mist.

Lights up on a still, posed figure, a man dressed circa eighteenth century. When lights are fully up he comes to life.

VOLTAIRE What a wonderful morning.

Absolutely wonderful. Très magnifique.

A morning when you wake up and think 'why, life is wonderful after all!'

You think of things like trees and the wind and your heart leaps

And as you shave you wonder if this is the dawn of a whole new age...

My name is Voltaire.

I am on holiday.

I can tell you I am having a lovely holiday.

I love England.

I love it to death.

But France I hate.

France I spit on.

France is enough to drive a man to live abroad!

Here you are so modern, so successful.

You have liberty and plumbing.

What has France got?

Lots of people who know what time the king gets up

What time he has a piss

Powders his wig and so on.

Here, you have killed your king

Whoop!

And off came his head

And that is not such a bad thing.

Fuck his wig, eh?

The world may laugh at you and say

Pah, the English, so ugly and they do not wash.

But that is because you are so busy doing lots of trade.

Then your nation gets richer and you get freer

And so you are more free to get rich etc.

Yes, in England you have cast out darkness and superstition and let the light of reason flood in.

Breakfast now. I'm hungry.

I tell you. I've seen the future and it works.

England.

FANNY HILL *has been lurking, dishevelled, in the background.*

FANNY Over here, Monsieur!

Have you an itch that needs a scratch?

VOLTAIRE Mon dieu!

He crosses himself. Exits.

FANNY French git!

I got nits off a Frenchie.

Nits are French, did you know that?

She begins to move, slowly, painfully.

It was cold last night.

Cold is bad for business.

Blokes don't like to tarry.

Frightened the frost will nobble their vitals.

No such luck.

Frost is after bigger catch.

Frost doesn't want a few sweaty fleshy inches.

Frost wants everything.

Hands, feet, legs, bum.

Frost is after the whole of Fanny.

Wants to fuck me over once and for all.

(shouts to frost) You're not having me!

Not the price you're asking!

Fanny's fallen on hard times. Hard times.

Corners aren't as dark as they used to be

And customers are fussy.

What I say is, you don't need teeth to give good suck!

I wish it was always dark.

Black like inside a hat.

Then I'd do business.

Then I'd have a carriage and a parrot.

I haven't eaten for three days.

I could be dead on Sunday!

Bugger!

A man enters.

Hark! A spark!

Maybe my luck has changed.

I'll keep to the shadows.

God bless him, he approaches.

(in a sweet voice) Morning, sir.

Have you a moment?

I need a hand for I am all unlaced.

SPARK I have reason to believe that you are the infamous Fanny Hill. Whore of this parish.

FANNY *(aside)* Lord, a constable!

   (to him) Me, sir! No, sir!

SPARK My informants are reliable...

FANNY There has been some abhorrent mix-up, officer, I may be out and about, sir, in these icy and sordid environs but I have a legitimate 'scuse. I am a widow of holy and reticent parts and as such I venture forth after morning prayers to walk my beloved pups. My husband, God, rest him, bred assorted canines.

SPARK Where are these pups?

FANNY Please, sir, it is a tragedy. As we veered into the vicinity of Hardudder Street, hearing a loud 'pop', I know not of what genesis, my two pups took fright and in their quivering distress, bit through their silken reigns and legged it.

SPARK Legged it?

FANNY Fled off – alas, such sweet and innocent doggies. The world may never see their like again. Turpin and Fudge I called 'em. One for it was black and fast, the other 'cos it was brown and slow.

   SPARK *pulls out a knife.*

SPARK See this?

FANNY A knife, sir.

SPARK It likes old flesh.

FANNY I've never so much as taken a boot to my doggies.

   He pushes it closer to her.

   Help!

SPARK Enough of your filthy conundrums.

   You are Fanny Hill. That tart on the turn.

FANNY I am, sir, but less of your turn.

SPARK A word.

FANNY Spit it out.

SPARK I have something about my person that will be of particular interest to you.

FANNY I doubt it.

SPARK Pardon.

FANNY A sneeze. Pray continue.

SPARK Notifications of debts. Gambling.

FANNY I abhor it. A woman that gambles is an iniquitous sight before man or God.

SPARK They've your signature.

FANNY Since we've that proved give 'em here.

SPARK They're mine.

FANNY Yours?

SPARK Purchased for a piddling sum. Their rightful owner having long given up hope of just recompense.

FANNY Miserable turd.

SPARK Now you owe me.

FANNY I understand.

My, we have come a long way round.

Well, what fleshy peculiarity are you after?

Which tickling trick that long and arduous service to my noble profession has endowed me?

Pause.

What do you want? Jam, thongs or catskins?

SPARK Back off, strumpet.

I'm talking business.

I have a proposition.

Scientific.

FANNY Go on.

SPARK A whore sells herself to one man at one time.

What if she could sell herself to fifty?

FANNY She'd never get up again.

SPARK One hundred. Simultaneous.

FANNY Impossible!

SPARK A thousand.

FANNY Exercrable!

SPARK Ten thousand!

FANNY I must stop my ears to such numerous and exhausting talk.

SPARK There is a way.

Pause.

I want you to write a book.

The story of your horrid career.

Thus servicing the multitude in one singular act.

FANNY How disgusting! A book.

SPARK Ten per cent on sales and we'll forget the debt.

FANNY Never. Books aren't meant for that sort of thing.

They're meant for educative purposes, holy instruction and genteel pastimes.

SPARK Fifteen per cent.

FANNY Done.

SPARK No double-crossing. Or I'll deliver the debts to the magistrate and you to Newgate. There's always room for one more trollop.

FANNY I'll start work immediately.

SPARK Remember. No prating tales of hardship and denials. Think of the customer.

FANNY I always do.

SPARK I'll be back.

FANNY You're too kind.

SPARK *flicks a coin onto the ground.*

SPARK An advance.

He leaves. She watches him go.

FANNY May your balls shrivel up and your cock drop off.

She picks up the coin and holds it up.

Money!

This is as if she has uttered a magic word. A group of three women gather round her as if entranced by the coin. They freeze. FANNY *breaks from the group. Comes forward. Speaks to the audience.*

I have a confession.

My horrid career.

It has been horrid I'm sure of that.

But when I turn round fast to catch at it all I see is a blur of bedpans, or a bloke buttoning up.

You see my past has seeped out the crack between the days.

Temporary, I'm sure.

It will be back but not in time, I fear.

Not much of a one for remembrances, me.

Been kept busy.

And what's a past 'cept rotten dragging longings and memories of bad paths badly trod.

What good's that do a girl?

There is others though, who shall help me.

If my past is missing I shall ask them to find one for me.

That way a story shall be told come what may.

And I will write my book.

And get a percentage, after.

She rejoins her pose with the group.

Lights up on LOUISA *and her.*

Louisa!

She tosses her a bottle.

I been looking for you.

LOUISA *swigs at the bottle.*

Louisa?

How's tricks?

LOUISA All right.

FANNY I've heard they've been better.

LOUISA No.

    Takes another swig.

FANNY It's hard.

    Pause.

    It's hard.

LOUISA What?

FANNY When you get a reputation.

LOUISA Reputation?

FANNY Unjust.

LOUISA Reputation?

FANNY People will talk.

LOUISA I'm fine.

FANNY Spread things.

LOUISA Fine.

Pause.

FANNY You worked in the theatre once.

LOUISA On the wigs. Combing 'em. Used to find all sorts.

FANNY But you understand the medium.

LOUISA Beetles. Mice even.

FANNY The art form.

LOUISA I left. The pay was crap.

FANNY I want your help.

LOUISA Help?

FANNY I want you to be me. Young and ravishably innocent as I was. Then you'll do things and I'll write 'em down.

LOUISA I dunno.

FANNY People talk talk talk. Louisa.

Things get round fast.

Makes it hard, keeping body and soul together.

LOUISA I want a sovereign.

FANNY You'll have one. We've got funding. Business sponsorship.

LOUISA *takes a swig.*

LOUISA I don't do anything without my friend.

She beckons SWALLOW *forward.*

FANNY What's her name?

LOUISA Dunno.

FANNY You could be mixing with all sorts.

SWALLOW Swallow.

FANNY What?

SWALLOW My name.

LOUISA She's new.

SWALLOW Like the bird.

LOUISA I met her on the streets.

SWALLOW I can read.

LOUISA She's got class.

SWALLOW There is garden in her face,
    Where roses and white lilies blow;
    A heavenly paradise is that place,
    Wherein all pleasant fruits do flow.

LOUISA That's poetry.

FANNY But no advantage.

    She gets a shilling.

LOUISA What do I do then?

FANNY Imagine.

LOUISA What?

FANNY It's London. One fine morning.

FIDDLE Excuse me...

FANNY At a coach station...

FIDDLE I'm ever so sorry to...

FANNY You're a young girl, scarce fifteen, newly arrived to the
    great metropolis.

    FIDDLE *plays a note on her violin to interrupt.*

FIDDLE I can play a wide variety of...

FANNY Sit over there.

FIDDLE Oh. Thank you. Um. I was wondering...

FANNY Sixpence.

FIDDLE Oh.

She seats herself with her violin. From now on she plays to accompany moments, scenes.

LOUISA I feel stupid.

FANNY Close your eyes.

LOUISA *does so. So does* **SWALLOW**.

You're all alone. Penniless.

An innocent and friendless orphan new to London.

What will happen?

Imagine.

Pause.

Well?

LOUISA I'll get screwed.

FANNY That is a trifle bald, Louisa.

LOUISA It's the truth.

FANNY But it lacks narrative.

The reader, as we all do, requires a little fondling before being brought to the point.

LOUISA Please yourself.

SWALLOW *comes forward. She has her eyes closed.*

SWALLOW Coming to the city is like I'm a flower picked and thrown into the street.

She opens her eyes.

I think I have feeling for it. Book writing. I've seen a book, you see. Touched it.

She closes her eyes again.

A flower or a fish that is flopped onto stone and is gasping.

FANNY Sweet bud, that is full of promise.

SWALLOW Or...

FANNY But quite enough to be going on with.

LOUISA How can it be like a flopping fish?

>FANNY *holds* SWALLOW's *face in her hands. Looks at it.*

FANNY There's a resemblance. You shall be the young Fanny.

LOUISA What about me?

FANNY You can fill in.

LOUISA Fill in?

FIDDLE A small role well played often gathers more acclaim than the star part from a discerning and sympathetic audience.

LOUISA Piss off.

FANNY (to FIDDLE) Yes. *(To* SWALLOW*)* Shall we begin, dear heart?

>SWALLOW *prepares herself.* LOUISA *watches antagonistically.* SWALLOW *looks about her, lost. Appears to be waiting. Sighs.*

SWALLOW/FANNY Left thus alone, in the heart of the throbbing cosmopolis, absolutely destitute and friendless I began to feel most bitterly the severity of my helpless strange circumstances and burst into a flood of tears.

FANNY Wonderful.

SWALLOW Thank you.

FANNY I will now enter the scene myself. Excuse me.

>FANNY *goes to find a piece of costume in order to play the madam. Perhaps she always finds pieces from about her person?*

SWALLOW Listening. That's how I got my education.

I worked for this bloke. He was a poet.

He had this sore on his leg.

It dripped on the floor where he sat.

I had to clean it up.

Sit under his table and clean it up.

I used my hanky.

FANNY *(from afar)* I'm nearly ready...

SWALLOW I used to hear him muttering, reading.

That's how I learnt things.

Wiping and listening.

Listening and wiping.

My hanky turned yellow.

FANNY *(calls)* Ready?

She enters.

FANNY/MOTHER BROWN Sweetheart. Do you want a place?

SWALLOW/FANNY Yes please.

FANNY/MOTHER BROWN What luck. I have come to this coach station in search of a servant.

And since I cannot bear to think of such an artless, inexperienced country maid wandering the streets of such a very vile wicked place as London you must come with me. I believe you might do, with a little instruction on my part.

SWALLOW/FANNY I will not hesitate to accept this offer of shelter especially from so grave and matron-like a lady.

FANNY/MOTHER BROWN Charming. This way.

They walk in a circle. FANNY *leads.* SWALLOW *follows.*

SWALLOW/FANNY My name is Fanny.

FANNY/MOTHER BROWN Indeed!

I've not taken you for the common type of servant, Fanny.

Not for scrubbing.

But, if you are a good girl, to be my companion.

I'll be twenty mothers to you.

SWALLOW/FANNY Twenty!

FANNY/MOTHER BROWN And you shall lie with a young gentlewoman, my cousin.

SWALLOW/FANNY Thank you!

(*to audience*) I was by the greatest good luck fallen into the hands of the kindest mistress, not to say friend, the varsal world could afford. I shall enter her doors with most complete confidence and exultation.

FANNY *stops.*

FANNY/MOTHER BROWN My abode.

(*calls out*) Phoebe! Phoebe! Phoebe!!!

LOUISA (*ungraciously*) I'm coming! I'm coming!

She enters the scene as **PHOEBE.** *She takes her time.*

LOUISA/PHOEBE Oh sweet mistress, it's you.

How glad I am that you have returned. Such a good sweet mistress.

FANNY/MOTHER BROWN Well, I'm for bed. I'm dog tired.

And I bet you are too, Phoebe.

LOUISA/PHOEBE Shagged.

FANNY/MOTHER BROWN This is the young gentlewoman I told you of, Fanny. She will show you the way and be vastly good to you, I'm sure.

Good night.

FANNY *retires to scribble.*

SWALLOW/FANNY Good night...

LOUISA *walks over to the bed.* **LOUISA** *had begun to take off some clothes.*

So. This is where we are to sleep.

It's a bit early. Not yet lunch time.

Pause. **SWALLOW** *begins to take off some clothes.*

LOUISA/PHOEBE Don't hang about.

SWALLOW/FANNY I have heard how several maids out of the country have made themselves forever by preserving their virtue and this so winning their masters that they married 'em and kept them coaches and they lived vastly grand and happy and some of them came to be duchesses.

I don't know how I will sleep.

SWALLOW *follows* **LOUISA** *to bed.*

Good night, Phoebe.

LOUISA/PHOEBE Good night, Fanny.

As they get into bed **LOUISA** *gives* **SWALLOW** *a kiss on the lips.*

SWALLOW/FANNY *(aside)* This was new. This was odd.

LOUISA *kisses her again.*

But not so bad.

Perhaps it is the London way to do things.

A way to show pure kindness.

I am such an unpractised simpleton perfectly new to life that such things are unknown to me.

Still, I will not be behind hand but return the embrace with all the fervour that innocence knows.

SWALLOW *kisses* **LOUISA** *back.*

A pause. **SWALLOW** *calls over to* **FANNY**.

SWALLOW Miss Fanny, what shall I do now?

FANNY Use your imagination and if you can't do that, think of your shilling.

They find a series of positions to illustrate this next speech. The positions change at intervals.

SWALLOW/FANNY Encouraged by this her hands became extremely free and wandered over my whole body with touches, squeezes...

FANNY Pressures

SWALLOW/FANNY ...pressures that rather warmed and surprised me with their novelty than shocked or alarmed me.

Every part of me was...

FANNY Open

SWALLOW/FANNY ...open and exposed to the licentious courses of her hands which like a fire ran over my whole body and thawed all coldness as they went.

Not content with the outer posts she now attempts the...

FANNY Main spot

SWALLOW/FANNY ...that sweet seat of exquisite sensation which till that instance had been quite innocent.

I should have jumped out of bed and cried 'help' against such odd assaults but her lascivious touches had lighted up a new fire, a strange pleasure that wantoned through all my veins, I was confused

FANNY Oh that's good

SWALLOW/FANNY Transported, out of myself...

A man enters.

DINGLE Hello.

Everything stops. They all look at the man.

Pause.

What are you doing?

LOUISA We're writing a book.

DINGLE Oh.

FANNY Any objections, sir, or may we continue unmolested with our literary activities?

DINGLE Don't mind me.

If I may make so bold I would like to introduce myself.

My name is Dingle.

FANNY Fanny Hill. You're standing in our best bedroom so to speak, Mr Dingle.

He jumps aside.

DINGLE I do beg your pardon.

LOUISA I seen him before. Hanging about like an old tooth.

DINGLE A man must take the air, miss.

FANNY We digress. Let us put Dingle in parenthesis and continue.

DINGLE Please. Don't do that. I wish to remain, Miss Fanny. May I?

LOUISA What for?

Pause.

DINGLE I would dearly love to learn the art of quill-driving.

FANNY That can be arranged.

DINGLE I'm indebted.

FANNY Precisely. Ten shillings.

DINGLE Ten shillings!

FANNY It's an educational experience.

DINGLE I am temporarily at a low ebb, so to speak.

FANNY How much?

DINGLE Tuppence and a piece of cork though that is slightly chewed.

FANNY Here.

She holds out her hand. He gives it to her.

You're on the slate.

DINGLE I have seen better days. I used to own half a ship.

LOUISA In a bottle.

DINGLE A regular sea-going vessel, Miss.

FANNY Returning to our incarnations of pleasure...young Fanny having had the first sparks of delight tossed onto her kindling is now rigged out to be a proper lady.

SWALLOW *swings around.*

SWALLOW A Brussels lace cap.

FANNY Braided shoes.

LOUISA Silk stockings.

FIDDLE A white lute-string flowered with silver.

DINGLE 'Tis a giddy age.

SWALLOW *stops.* **FANNY** *arranges her more revealingly. They look as if into a mirror. The others hold still.*

FANNY I was barely turned fifteen.

My shape owed nothing to stays.

My hair was glossy, flowing down my back in natural buckles and not a little setting off the whiteness of a smooth skin.

My eyes were as black as can be imagined

And my bosom finely raised, though one might discern rather the promise than the actuality of the firm round breasts that would soon make good.

This is, I own, strong self-praise, but should I not show gratitude to nature?

Why suppress, through affectations of modesty, the mention of such valuable gifts?

Plus, a reader likes things fleshed out.

The others reanimate.

I'm sure you're keen to assist us, Dingle.

DINGLE　If it is an honest book, Miss Fanny.

FANNY　Sir, 'tis the stark naked truth.

FANNY/MOTHER BROWN　Fanny, sweetness?

SWALLOW/FANNY　Yes, Mother Brown?

FANNY/MOTHER BROWN　You look plums in sugar today.

Allow me to introduce to you my esteemed coz. Mr Crofts.

She indicates **DINGLE***. He bows his head.*

A very fine gentleman.

Isn't that right, Phoebe?

LOUISA/PHOEBE　Yeah. Very fine.

FANNY/MOTHER BROWN　Not above sixty and with his own chariot.

More, he is violently smitten with you at first sight.

DINGLE *stares at* **SWALLOW***. A pause.*

Now Phoebe and I must leave on pressing business.

Farewell.

They start to leave.

SWALLOW/FANNY　Wait!

He is looking at me goats and monkeys.

FANNY/MOTHER BROWN As I said. Important business.

SWALLOW/FANNY He is staring at my bosom.

FANNY/MOTHER BROWN Sir, be very tender of the sweet child.

Phoebe!

They exit. **DINGLES** *stares at* **SWALLOW**. *She is uncomfortable.*

SWALLOW/FANNY Alone!

I stole corner glances at him, then looked away in pure horror and affright, which he attributed to nothing more than maiden modesty.

DINGLE *gives a grotesque smile.*

DINGLE/MR CROFTS Come over here poppet.

SWALLOW/FANNY No you are a liquorish old goat.

Imagine a short ugly man who looks...dead.

And had great goggly eyes as if he were being strangled.

Fangs.

Breath like a lavvy.

And when he smiled it was horrible if not downright dangerous to a woman with child.

DINGLE *breaks out of character.*

DINGLE You can't put that in!

SWALLOW/FANNY He lavished great sums on such wretches as could pretend to love his person whilst to those who had not the art to dissemble he behaved brutally.

DINGLE It's slander!

SWALLOW/FANNY He thought he was born to please women, though he could best please them by his extinction.

DINGLE Scurrilous libel!

FANNY Advance, Dingle!

> **DINGLE,** *back in character, moves towards* **SWALLOW.** *She attempts to avoid him.* **DINGLE** *stumbles after. He may grab hold of her but does not have an easy time of it.*

> **FANNY** *writes.*

SWALLOW/FANNY The monster flings his arms about my neck, draws me forcibly towards him and obliges me to receive his pestilential kisses. He tears off my handkerchief and pushes me to the settee. I feel his hand on my naked thighs which are crossed and which he endeavours to unlock. Oh, then! Aroused out of my passive endurance I sprung from him with an activity he was not prepared for, flung myself at his feet and begged him Do not hurt me, Mr Crofts.

DINGLE/MR CROFTS Hurt you?

SWALLOW/FANNY I shall love you dearly...if you go away!

DINGLE/MR CROFTS Saucebox!

SWALLOW/FANNY I am talking to the wind.

DINGLE/MR CROFTS Hurt you?

SWALLOW/FANNY The disorder of my dress proves fresh incentive. Snorting and foaming...

> *He snorts and foams.*

DINGLE/MR CROFTS AND SWALLOW/FANNY With lust and rage...

SWALLOW/FANNY He seizes me and tosses my petticoats over my head.

> *She gives a cry. Struggles.*

I struggle with indignation! I died with terror!

DINGLE/MR CROFTS I am unbuttoned!

> **DINGLE** *goes to close in with a final lunge.* **SWALLOW** *rolls over/moves. He misses. He collapses with a cry of dismay.*

A silence.

SWALLOW *sits up.*

SWALLOW/FANNY He had it seems, brought on, by his eagerness and struggle, the ultimate period of his hot fit of lust, which his power was too short-lived to carry him through the full execution of.

FANNY He came too soon.

DINGLE Strumpet.

SWALLOW It's all over my petticoat.

DINGLE/MR CROFTS Country modesty! I know what's second-hand goods. You've left your maidenhead with some village hobnail and come to dispose of your skim-milk in town!

FANNY Louisa, fetch Mr Dingle some refreshment.

He's in need of protein to perk-ify his performance.

LOUISA *gets a gin bottle. Swigs it herself.*

SWALLOW My petticoat…

FANNY It'll dry out.

SWALLOW *sits dabbing her petticoat.*

(to **FIDDLE***)* A little mood music, I think.

In order to succour my scribbling.

FIDDLE *complies.*

FANNY Funny. I keep 'xpecting some sound, some sight; the toss of a petticoat or a groan perhaps, to jog my memory.

To slip me my past.

But no.

Still, early days.

FIDDLE Early days.

FANNY *writes.*

DINGLE Miss... Louisa?

LOUISA What?

DINGLE That was the name of my ship.

LOUISA What?

DINGLE Louisa.

Pause.

A good ship. She sailed remarkably fast.

You could send her to sea at easy expense.

First I only had one sixteenth of her.

Then I saved and saved till I had a whole half.

A whole half.

Don't take me wrong, Miss Louisa.

There was a woman on the front of my ship.

She was made of wood. She had two big blue eyes.

Mind you, she only had a top half. No legs.

Her mouth was red.

She looked like you.

LOUISA She was made of wood?

DINGLE Oak.

LOUISA Even her tits?

DINGLE I never looked.

LOUISA They must have been.

DINGLE I never looked.

LOUISA She would've got cold. All them waves, splashing her. She must have thought of you, all snug and tucked up at night. And her. Freezing.

DINGLE She wasn't alive.

LOUISA Not like me.

DINGLE No.

LOUISA No. She was hard, whereas me, I'm soft.

Wood tits aren't as good as the real thing.

DINGLE Miss Louisa!

She laughs.

SWALLOW *(to* **FANNY***)* One day he found me.

The bloke I worked for.

Touching his book.

He was a gentleman though.

He didn't scold me.

He read me a poem.

There cherries grow which none may buy

Till 'cherry-ripe' themselves do cry.

FANNY Enchanting. I can see you've a flare.

SWALLOW A flare?

FANNY For books.

SWALLOW I have?

FANNY I'd say.

SWALLOW Is Mr Crofts coming back?

FANNY No, dear heart. He has been incarcerated for illegal contraband practices.

SWALLOW Oh, good.

FANNY Ever onwards, else our readers will be salivating themselves for chapter two: 'The Mysteries of Venus'.

An intro on the violin.

LOUISA *(sings)*

THERE IS A THING LONG AND STIFF

AND AT THE END THERE IS A CLIFF
SOFT MOISTURE FROM IT DOTH GROW
AND MAKES FAIR LADIES PLEASANT GROW.

SWALLOW What is it?

LOUISA A pen.

DINGLE You've got a nice voice, Louisa.

FANNY It's twelve midnight. The shutters are down. The house is quiet. Young Fanny and Phoebe happen to be in Mother Brown's closet, when they hear a rustling in the bed chamber.

She makes sounds of rustling.

SWALLOW What's that?

LOUISA It is a rustling in the bed chamber.

> **FANNY** *draws a curtain round the bed. Lights focus on this.* **LOUISA** *and* **SWALLOW** *go one either side of the curtain.*

LOUISA/PHOEBE We instantly crept softly and posted ourselves so that...

SWALLOW/FANNY Seeing everything minutely...

LOUISA/PHOEBE ...**We could not been seen.**

They draw the curtain back or it is drawn back.

SWALLOW/FANNY Then who should we see but the venerable mother abbess herself with a tall, brawny, young horse grenadier...

LOUISA/PHOEBE ...**moulded in the Hercules style.**

We see **FANNY** *with* **SPARK** *disguised as a horse grenadier. He should be partly masked so as not to become a 'real' character. They pose.*

LOUISA/PHOEBE AND SWALLOW/FANNY Oh, how still and hush did we keep our stands...

The pose breaks. A purse is exchanged. They go straight to work. A dumbshow is enacted. Music accompanies this.

SONG: "WHEN FOR AIR I TAKE MY MARE"

WHEN FOR AIR I TAKE MY MARE

LOUISA/PHOEBE They got straight down to essentials.
AND MOUNT HER FIRST SHE WALKS JUST THUS

SWALLOW/FANNY Her face blushed—

LOUISA/PHOEBE With brandy.
HER HEAD HELD LOW HER MOTION SLOW
WITH NODDING, PLODDING, WAGGING, JOGGING
DASHING, PLASHING, SNORTING, STARTING,
WHIMSICALLY SHE GOES.

SWALLOW/FANNY But soon I stared with all my eyes at a thing that entirely engrossed them...

LOUISA/PHOEBE Her sturdy stallion had now unbuttoned and produced...

SWALLOW/FANNY And produced...his willy.

FANNY interrupts.

FANNY And produced that wonderful machine, that treasure.

LOUISA/PHOEBE That piece of furniture.

FANNY That flesh brush, capital part and beloved guest.

LOUISA Bit of gristle.

FANNY That maypole, pleasure wedge, love truncheon, plenipotentiary instrument and is someone taking notes?

DINGLE hurries in to do so.

DINGLE Sorry.

Dumbshow continues.
THEN WHIP STIRS UP, TROT, TROT, TROT, TROT;

AMBLING THEN WITH EASY SLIGHT,
SHE WRIGGLES LIKE A BRIDE AT NIGHT;
HER SHUFFLING HITCH, REGALES MY BRITCH;
WHILST TROT, TROT, TROT, TROT,
BRINGS ON THE GALLOP, THE GALLOP, THE GALLOP,
THE GALLOP, AND THEN A SHORT TROT,
TROT, TROT, TROT,
STRAIGHT AGAIN UP AND DOWN, UP AND DOWN, UP AND
    DOWN
TILL SHE COMES HOME WITH A TROT
WHEN THE NIGHT DARK GROWS.

JUST SO PHILLIS, FAIR AS LILLIES,
AS HER FACE IS, HAS HER PACES
AND IN BED TOO, LIKE MY PAD TOO;
NODDING, PLODDING, WAGGING, JOGGING;
DASHING, PLASHING, FLIRTING, SPURTING,
ARTFUL ARE HER WAYS:
HEART THUMPS PITT, PATT, TROT, TROT, TROT, TROT
AMBLING THEN HER TONGUE GETS LOOSE,
WHILST WRIGGLING NEAR I PRESS FULL CLOSE:
YE DEVIL SHE CRIES, I'LL TEAR YOUR EYES,
WHEN MAIN SEIZ'D, BUM SQUEEZ'D
I GALLOP, I GALLOP, I GALLOP, I GALLOP,
I GALLOP, AND THEN I TROT,
TROT, TROT, TROT
STRAIGHT AGAIN UP AND DOWN, UP AND DOWN, UP AND
    DOWN,
TILL THE LAST JERK WITH A TROT
ENDS OUR LOVE CHASE.

They let the curtain drop.

LOUISA/PHOEBE We were thrilled

SWALLOW/FANNY to the soul

LOUISA/PHOEBE and our emotions had grown

SWALLOW/FANNY so violent

LOUISA/PHOEBE that they almost intercepted our respiration.

They breathe out heavily.

SWALLOW/FANNY Such a sight had given the dying blow to my native innocence.

She approaches **LOUISA.**

Now I am all stirred up and aglow with stimulating fires.

As she goes to embrace **LOUISA,** **FANNY** *steps between them, through the curtain and separates them.*

FANNY But young Fanny was pining for more solid food and would not be put off much longer with this foolery of woman to woman.

SWALLOW Oh.

LOUISA Please yourself.

FANNY It's not what gentlemen read books for.

I thought you had a feeling for books.

SWALLOW I do.

FANNY I might have mistook you.

SWALLOW No.

FANNY We're writing for a market.

DINGLE Herrings.

FANNY How's that, Mr Dingle?

DINGLE It's no good shipping herrings to the Spanish, Miss Fanny. They have an aversion.

FANNY Quite so. Shall we tilt our prow at the ensuing scenario?

I have made notes.

She reads. **SWALLOW** *sits centre stage.*

I wanted no more of Phoebe. Everything there so flat, so hollow... I'd only obliged before out of fear of displeasing her...but now, for my part, I was filled with ardent desires for the main dish, the essential specific!

SWALLOW Ardent desires for the essential specific...

FANNY Exactly!

> **SWALLOW** *looks about her. Fetches a coat. The space clears. She is left alone.* **FANNY** *looks on. Lights focus on* **SWALLOW**. *She looks at the coat.*

SWALLOW/FANNY An eye.

Two eyes.

Eyelashes.

Red lips like a bee has stung them.

Curly hair.

All disordered.

Heavens what a sight!

A boy.

A young gentleman.

He is fast asleep in Mother Brown's chair.

Left there by his thoughtless companions who got him drunk, dumped him and went off for a screw.

Trembling, I took one of his hands in mine and woke him as gentle as possible.

What time is it, he asks?

Six o'clock, I replied.

His eyes had fire in them.

I could not help it but I touched his cheek.

He kissed me.

It was the first kiss I had ever relished from a man in all my life.

Pause.

Love.

Pause.

Love.

SONG: "OH! MY PANTING HEART"

OH MY PANTING, PANTING HEART,

WHY SO YOUNG, AND WHY SO SAD?

WHY DOES PLEASURE SEEM A SMART,

OR I WRETCHED WHILE I'M GLAD?

OH! LOVERS GODDESS, WHO WERT FORM'D,

FROM COLD AND ICY, ICY SEAS;

INSTRUCT ME WHY I AM THUS WARM'D,

AND DARTS AT ONCE CAN WOUND AND PLEASE.

His names was... Charles.

FANNY Charles?

SWALLOW/FANNY Yes.

FANNY Who the hell's Charles?

> *They all gather round.* **SWALLOW** *stays sitting in the middle of them, looking up.*

SWALLOW/FANNY A gentleman.

FANNY Gentleman?

SWALLOW/FANNY I'm in love.

FANNY Oh yes?

SWALLOW/FANNY Yes. I've escaped with him. He asked if he could keep me.

FANNY And then what?

SWALLOW/FANNY Nothing. We are very happy.

FANNY And that's it?

SWALLOW/FANNY That's it.

FANNY 'I was very happy and that's it.'

    I can't write that.

SWALLOW/FANNY We are happy.

FANNY You can't end a book on chapter three.

    Too thin. It wouldn't sell.

    He'll have to go.

SWALLOW/FANNY No.

FANNY Yes.

SWALLOW/FANNY No.

DINGLE Perhaps he could be struck on the head by a blunt object whilst strolling on the dock side. He would then fall into the waters and drown without ever regaining consciousness.

SWALLOW/FANNY No.

LOUISA He could choke on a crust.

SWALLOW/FANNY No.

FIDDLE Or be gored by a stray bullock.

SWALLOW/FANNY He was to come back. I'm having his baby.

    Pause.

FANNY How did that happen?

SWALLOW/FANNY We loved each other.

FANNY How?

SWALLOW/FANNY You know.

FANNY Did it hurt?

SWALLOW/FANNY No.

FANNY Not even the first time?

    That's funny. It usually hurts the first time.

Doesn't it Louisa?

LOUISA I've had worse.

SWALLOW/FANNY A little. Perhaps it hurt a little.

LOUISA Best to stuff your petticoat in your mouth and bite down hard.

FIDDLE Or recite a rhyme.

FANNY It hurts but they do it. They go ahead and do it.

Don't they, Mr Dingle?

DINGLE That is God's will, Miss Fanny.

FANNY It would be.

SWALLOW/FANNY Charles was very kind.

FANNY Oh, I can see it all.

Come, come, my dear, says he.

Let me show you a room with a fine prospect over some gardens...

But we know what prospects he had in mind. He starts the main attack...

SWALLOW/FANNY I told him my flower was yet uncropped.

FANNY He shoves it in.

SWALLOW/FANNY I tell him I cannot bear it.

FANNY So he gives it a grease...

SWALLOW/FANNY He kisses my falling tears.

FANNY And carries on. He breaks in, carrying all before him and with one violent merciless lunge sends his pole imbrued and reeking with virgin gore right up the very hilt of you. Charming.

SWALLOW/FANNY But Charles employed such warmth to soothe, caress and comfort me even bringing me a cordial, that presently I drowned all sense of pain in the pleasure of seeing him, of thinking I belonged to him, he who was the absolute dispenser of my happiness, my fate.

FANNY I bet he wanted to try again in five minutes.

LOUISA I lost mine off a young gentleman of the cleaver.

FIDDLE I beg your pardon?

LOUISA A butcher.

> **FANNY** *indicates that she is about to start work again. The others leave centre stage.*

FANNY/MRS JONES Well, now, young Fanny. I am your present landlady. Mrs Jones. I'm come to give you some news. I doubt you will ever set eyes on Charles again.

SWALLOW/FANNY No!

FANNY/MRS JONES A jealous relative has had him bundled abroad a ship headed for the south seas. Tragic. These voyages can be highly perilous and the native women most flirtatious.

> **FANNY** *tosses the coat aside.* **LOUISA** *grabs it.*

LOUISA Oh, Charles!

SWALLOW/FANNY What about the baby?

FANNY You lose it.

> **SWALLOW** *gives a small cry.*

SWALLOW/FANNY No...

> *She sinks to the floor.*

FANNY Art requires sacrifice.

You may call me hard-hearted but I merely place myself upon the altar of literature.

An encumbered heroine is a sentimental liability, especially in a book of the *œuvre*.

She turns to **SWALLOW**.

FANNY/MRS JONES Your health is returning to you even as I speak. You are welcome to stay in these lodgings as long as you please, Miss Fanny, but you owe me twenty-three pounds and seventeen and six pence and I would not like to see you rot in Newgate.

SWALLOW/FANNY Newgate?

FANNY/MRS JONES *You must eat.*

SWALLOW/FANNY I'm not hungry.

FANNY/MRS JONES Nonsense. When you've got down half a partridge and four glasses of wine you'll feel much better.

SWALLOW/FANNY I've a melancholy.

FANNY/MRS JONES Sorrow passes.

Besides. I have a gentleman to visit you.

Mr H as he wishes to be known.

He has a large diamond ring and has heard of your misfortunes and is willing to serve you.

SWALLOW/FANNY I don't want to see anybody.

FANNY/MRS JONES This is no time for personal preferences.

Make your market while you may.

I'll send him up.

Try to look a little cheerful.

DINGLE *is ushered in.*

DINGLE/MR H Good afternoon.

I have heard of your terrible misfortune and have come to visit you.

Where shall I put my clothes? Have you got any hangers?

He begins to take off his clothes.

SWALLOW/FANNY I am lifeless.

DINGLE/MR H You'll feel differently in a day or two.

SWALLOW/FANNY I do not care what becomes of my wretched body.

DINGLE/MR H You say that now...

SWALLOW/FANNY I don't care if I die.

DINGLE/MR H Do you want your ten shillings or not?

A pause.

They begin a dumbshow of intercourse.

FANNY My! How the animal spirits do rush mechanically to their parts!

SWALLOW *(whispers)* Drink to me only with thine eyes,

And I will pledge with mine;

Or leave a kiss but in the cup

And I'll not look for wine.

By now the whole scene has faded.

FIDDLE There are not, on earth at least, eternal griefs.

Some are, if not at an end, at least suspended.

She gives a flourish on her violin.

Activity. **SWALLOW** *jumps up.* **FANNY** *hands a loop on a stick (a peep-hole prop).*

SWALLOW/FANNY I am now some seven months with Mr H.

And am kept in comfort and style.

One day I return from visiting...

She mimes returning.

I enter without knocking.

She enters.

Fancying I heard my maid's voice, I stole softly to the door which afforded a very commanding peep-hole.

She lifts up the hand held peep-hole. As she does so DINGLE *and* LOUISA *take up their positions.*

And there I see Mr H pulling and hauling at this coarse country strammel.

The tableau comes to life.

LOUISA/MAID Pray, sir, don't, sir. Let me alone. I am not for your turn. Sure, you cannot demean yourself with such a poor body as I? Lord, sir, my mistress may come home, I must not indeed. I will cry out.

Pause.

I think it will be easier if I sit on the table.

She sits on the 'table', pulls him towards her and makes very short work of him. She pushes him away, takes some money from his pocket...

Supper at seven then...sir.

She curtsies. Swaggers off. He attempts to recompose himself. Staggers off.

SWALLOW/FANNY This was provocation!

Only revenge could restore me to perfect composure.

She tosses aside the peep-hole.

Mr H had taken into his service a very handsome young lad. Scarce turned nineteen, as pretty a piece of women's meat as you were likely to see.

LOUISA *appears on cue. Dressed as a boy.*

His chief employment was to carry letters between his master and me.

LOUISA/SERVANT BOY Morning.

SWALLOW/FANNY Hitherto I had only taken notice of the comeliness of his youth, but now I began to look on him as a delicious instrument of my revenge

LOUISA/SERVANT BOY Here's your letter.

LOUISA holds out a letter.

SWALLOW/FANNY I could not help observing that this lad eyed me in a bashful, confused way. My figure it seems has struck him.

She takes the letter provocatively, screws it into a ball and throws it some distance.

I have dropped it.

LOUISA/SERVANT BOY You have dropped it.

LOUISA picks it up and attempts to smooth it out. She awkwardly hands it back. SWALLOW does not take it.

SWALLOW/FANNY Boy, have you a mistress?

LOUISA shakes her head, no.

Is she prettier than me?

LOUISA shakes her head, no.

Has she got smaller feet?

A pause.

Are you afraid of a lady?

She takes LOUISA's hand and places it on her breast.

A pause. They go to kiss and at that moment FANNY tosses something into the scene that rattles on the floor and breaks the moment. It is a sock.

LOUISA What's that?

FANNY What's it look like?

It's a representation, Louisa.

You've seen plenty of these before.

LOUISA Not like that I haven't.

FANNY It's the sceptre-member. Now get on with it.

LOUISA *puts it on her forearm.*

SWALLOW/FANNY I stole my hand upon his thighs...

Down one of which I could feel a stiff, hard body.

LOUISA/SERVANT BOY The essential object of enjoyment.

SWALLOW/FANNY Eager to unfold so alarming a mystery, I played with his buttons.

LOUISA/SERVANT BOY Which were bursting ripe with the active force within.

SWALLOW/FANNY When lo! His foreflap flew open at a touch...

LOUISA *picks it up and holds it up.*

LOUISA/SERVANT BOY And out it started!

SWALLOW/FANNY And I saw with wonder a maypole of so excessive a standard that had the proportions been observed it might have belonged to a young giant.

LOUISA *holds up the sock again.*

LOUISA/SERVANT BOY It was fucking enormous.

SWALLOW/FANNY And set off by a sprout of black curling hair at the root. Through which the fair skin showed as in a fine evening the clear light shows through the distant branch work of trees o'er topping the summit of a hill.

LOUISA/SERVANT BOY He had nice pubes.

SWALLOW/FANNY I made myself as open as possible.

Oh, how it did batter and bore against me

Stiffly, in random pushes, now above, now below its point.

DINGLE Careful!

SWALLOW/FANNY Battering and boring.

DINGLE Miss Fanny, I protest!

FANNY calls from offside.

FANNY Till burning with impatience I guided him gently in for his first lesson of pleasure.

SWALLOW/FANNY A favourable motion from me...

LOUISA/SERVANT BOY Met a timely thrust of his and so he gained lodgement.

SWALLOW/FANNY At the height of fury I twisted my legs around his and drew him home and kept him fast as if I sought to unite our two bodies.

LOUISA/SERVANT BOY And soon...

SWALLOW/FANNY I employed all the forwarding arts I knew to promote his keeping my company to the journey's end.

FANNY What did you do?

LOUISA/SERVANT BOY She squeezed his globular appendages.

FANNY That's my girl.

LOUISA/SERVANT BOY And then the symptoms of sweet agony!

LOUISA/SERVANT BOY AND SWALLOW/FANNY The melting moment...

FANNY Alliteration!

LOUISA/SERVANT BOY AND SWALLOW/FANNY Of dissolution when pleasure dies by pleasure...

FANNY Repetition.

LOUISA/SERVANT BOY AND SWALLOW/FANNY And flings us into an ecstasy breathless panting writhing...

FANNY Onomatopoeia.

LOUISA/SERVANT BOY AND SWALLOW/FANNY Then the hot warm floods

FANNY Metaphor, enjambment.

LOUISA/SERVANT BOY AND SWALLOW/FANNY And after, voluptuous, fast lock in arms languor.

FANNY Assonance!!!

Pause.

That's fucking poetry.

LOUISA/SERVANT BOY Soon we were ready to try again.

DINGLE No! Louisa!

This is too much.

This book, Miss Fanny!

FANNY Is coming on apace, Mr Dingle.

DINGLE But who will read it?

FANNY Those that can pay good money for it.

LOUISA/SERVANT BOY Once again I advanced...

SWALLOW *mimics* **LOUISA**'s *movement.*

DINGLE Louisa! I hear Mr H returning!

SWALLOW/FANNY I reach out...

DINGLE/MR H His foot is on the stair...

LOUISA/SERVANT BOY We embraced.

Both **SWALLOW** *and* **LOUISA** *are miming an embrace.*

DINGLE/MR H He is returned! He is returned!

DINGLE *assumes* **MR H**'s *character.*

SWALLOW/FANNY I screamed.

She screams.

And dropped my petticoat.

LOUISA/SERVANT BOY The thunderstruck lad stood trembling and pale.

SWALLOW/FANNY We stood before him like criminals.

DINGLE/MR H What have you to say for yourself?

To abuse me in such an unworthy manner and with my own servant. How have I deserved this?

SWALLOW/FANNY I have only done what you have done.

I had not a single thought in wrong doing you till I saw you taking liberties with my own serving wench last Tuesday.

That has driven me to this course which I do not pretend to justify.

This young man is faultless.

I seduced him to make him the instrument of my revenge.

His is innocent and I am guilty and entirely at your mercy.

DINGLE/MR H Madam, I take shame to myself and confess that you have fairly turned the tables on me. I own too that your clearing of this rascal here is just and honest in you.

However, there can be no comparison between my provocation and yours, for I am a gentleman and you are a tart.

And so, renew with you, madam, I cannot!

SWALLOW/FANNY But...

DINGLE/MR H The affront is too gross.

You've got a day to get out.

SWALLOW/FANNY Very well.

DINGLE/MR H And give me that.

He takes the sock.

This is my sock and it has been most vilely ill-used. Goodbye.

He exits. LOUISA *follows him.*

SWALLOW/FANNY I am once more adrift.

Cast out into a world cold, hard and bargaining.

What will become of me?

Alas, I have nothing...but fifty silver guineas.

And any woman of pleasure knows how little long that may last her...

SWALLOW *wanders to the sidelines.*

FANNY *is scribbling.*

FIDDLE I had a thought.

FANNY *continues to write.*

If I need to remember things I usually tie a knot in something.

She indicates her skirt which has a knot in it.

A knot. To remind me.

To help me remember.

I tie a knot in something.

A pause.

FIDDLE *coughs. She exits.*

FANNY *is scribbling.*

LOUISA I need my money.

I need it now. Today.

My sovereign.

You promised.

Pause.

I need it later then.

Later.

But I need it.

She begins to exit.

DINGLE *catches up with her.*

DINGLE Miss Louisa!

A pause.

There was a wild night once.

Wind and a storm.

A heavy sea.

My ship.

So much water in the sea.

Soon she became waterlogged.

So light but she became waterlogged.

All hands on ship! Someone shouted.

But still she sank like a weight.

That was a dark night.

LOUISA You wanted comforting.

DINGLE I did need comfort.

LOUISA Still, I expect you couldn't afford it then, eh?

She leaves. He follows.

SWALLOW I sat under the table, wiping.

I used to like listening.

Poetry. Beautiful. Nice.

The shepherd swains shall dance and sing

For thy delight each May morning;

If these delights thy mind may move,

Then live with me and be my love.

SPARK *comes on. Watches her.* **SWALLOW** *regards him with alarm.*

She runs off.

FANNY *scribbles.* **SPARK** *taps his cane on her table.*

FANNY It's you. What an unlooked for pleasure.

SPARK I was just passing.

FANNY We're half way.

SPARK Speedy work.

FANNY I've learnt never to entertain time-wasting necessaries, like excess biographical material or knickers.

SPARK Most commendable. When can I have my book?

FANNY You can't hurry art.

SPARK Oh, I'm not so sure.

Art, like everything, must have one eye cocked on the market. And if the market looks your way, it's a chaste soul that can refuse its goodly embrace.

Indeed t'would be unnatural!

For an appetite is a healthy thing.

And appetites must be fed.

FANNY I griddle as fast as I can.

Soon I will be out of paper!

SPARK Write smaller.

I will return.

FANNY I await you in breathless expectation.

He exits.

His book. His book.

It's my book. Mine.

Oh, I can see myself opulent.

Money. No more ice nights.

No more vomit stinking gobs and poxy pricks.

No.

He may be a driblet of dung but his idea's priceless.

Priceless and I'm having it.

My book. Mine. Mine.

Pause.

So far six fucks.

That's more than most of you get in an evening.

She puts down her pen.

Lights down.

Part Two

The violin plays. The whole cast are in a tableau of copulating, bizarre. It moves as one thing, like a machine. It gets frantic and then dies. Everyone 'dies' together. The machine collapses, sags. FANNY *speaks.*

FANNY Dear reader,

I imagined you would have been a trifle tired, nay, cloyed, with the uniformity of adventures and expressions inseparable from a subject of this sort.

But no.

Here you are returned for book two.

You may well be duller than I thought

And unable to concoct better for yourselves.

Poor lambs.

Still, you will appreciate my problem.

A certain repetition is inevitable.

And let's face it those awful words,

Joys, ardours, ecstasies, et cetera employed so regular in the practice of pleasure tend, like an old mattress to flatten with frequency and lose all bounce.

As Rousseau said a thousand times it is by the imagination alone that the senses are awakened. It will give colour to words worn thin by frequent handling.

As for the mincing metaphors and affected circumlocutions I employ to describe that old last act, don't blame me.

I am merely avoiding the whip of the censor which you, the darling public, have erected for your own moral protection.

Look at me now, speechifying.

I must obey my own rules

And immediately grab hold of the main parts of my story.

She reaches over and grabs DINGLE *by the crotch. He responds with an expression half pain/half pleasure. Simultaneously we hear a long note from the violin.*

Tempus fugit, Mr Dingle.

Are you with us?

DINGLE I think I may stay, Miss Fanny.

A voyage once embarked upon should not be lightly abandoned.

LOUISA *turns round. We see that she is heavily pregnant.*

SWALLOW Louisa!

FIDDLE Louisa!

DINGLE Louisa!

FANNY What fast work.

DINGLE Who's is it?

LOUISA Yours

DINGLE Mine!

LOUISA Wretch! Pisspot! Rascal!

DINGLE There's been some mistake.

LOUISA You treat a poor girl so!

DINGLE Upon my life, Miss Fanny...

LOUISA I am undone!

DINGLE I swear.

LOUISA Dog-breath. Will you not even pay for the upkeep?

She holds out her hand.

DINGLE Pay?

LOUISA Shag-bag. Villain. Pimp. I will call a constable.

DINGLE I beg you...

> LOUISA *laughs. She pulls a pillow out from under her skirt.*

LOUISA An easy birth.

SWALLOW Louisa...

LOUISA I've been earning a few dirty and dishonest pence down Sadler's Wells. Gulling a few culls.

DINGLE A swindling trade.

LOUISA Yeah.

FANNY Come come. Enough chattering.

I hear the muse calling.

LOUISA When am I going to get bleedin' paid?

I need it, soon, my sovereign.

FANNY In good time. In good time.

(to SWALLOW*)* Are you ready my sweetling?

An instrumental note.

SWALLOW/FANNY I am all alone in the world.

The streets smell of piss.

FANNY/MRS COLE Good evening.

May I introduce myself? I am Mrs Cole.

A middle-aged, discreet sort of woman.

May I offer you my cordial advice?

There is no one more acquainted with the wicked part of town than I.

So who is fitter to guard and advise you than I?

SWALLOW/FANNY Well...

FANNY/MRS COLE No one.

I keep a house of conveniency.

Promoting schemes of pleasure and unbounded debauchery.

However, I content myself with a moderate profit.

I am a gentlewoman born and bred, reduced to this course through dire necessity.

And the delight in encouraging a brisk circulation in the trade.

Here is my card.

We've a Covent Garden address you'll see, and only serve customers of distinction,

No turds.

Au revoir.

SWALLOW *accepts the card. Looks at it then at the audience.*

SWALLOW/FANNY Thus I passed from a private devotee of pleasure to a public one.

Thereafter being able to dispose of myself for the general good of all.

FANNY/MRS COLE *(aside as herself)* A natural market expansion.

(to **SWALLOW***)* Welcome.

We sit in the window here, see.

FIDDLE, FANNY, LOUISA, *all sit in a row as if facing a window. They are all sewing a large sheet. Dingle does the scripting in this scene.*

Demurely employed on millenary work.

A cover for traffic in more precious commodities.

SWALLOW *takes her place amongst them.* **LOUISA** *whistles.*

LOUISA Here's a spark!

They all pose and smile. They watch him pass in unison. Then the pose immediately drops indicating that he has passed by.

(calling after him) Mule's dropping!

FANNY/MRS COLE We do not sit idle.

But innocently imagine ourselves at a finishing school for fashionable young ladies. I the mistress of these young minds, these my pupils.

ALL Yes ma am.

FANNY/MRS COLE We practice the art of convivial conversation. For witty repartee is a highly prized quality in your courtesan, as is singing.

LOUISA As well as a most consummate skill in reviving the dead member

FIDDLE Is that a religious observance?

LOUISA It's a blow job.

FANNY/MRS COLE Yesterday we discoursed upon 'the amorous art of strangulation'.

LOUISA I had a fucking weirdo once.

FANNY/MRS COLE Louisa!

LOUISA He could only come if he watched me naked strangling a pigeon. I told him I hope you brought your own pigeon.

FANNY/MRS COLE Today our topic shall be 'the beasts of the field'.

FIDDLE Is there anything more delightful to the mind as keen instruction?

FANNY/MRS COLE Indeed no. I have heard tell of one Reverent Tiberius Dimple who succumbed to the attractions of a cow. He was sent to Newgate for two years but the cow was acquitted.

LOUISA She'd had her punishment.

FIDDLE   Perhaps we could discourse upon how to prevent the admittance of blunt and dangerous implements into the boudoir.

LOUISA   What? Please enter but leave your dick on the doormat?

FIDDLE   Hammers, I meant, or knives...

FANNY   Please. These are unsavoury practicalities and likely to snag at a smooth read.

FANNY/MRS COLE   I suggest 'when first we changed the maiden state for womanhood'. Louisa. May we have your story, dearest?

FANNY prompts her.

You came from a farming family, remember?

LOUISA   Oh yeah.

FANNY   But your parents didn't like you a bit, so they chucked you out.

LOUISA   Oh yeah.

FANNY   You took the road to London. After twelve miles you stopped in weariness and bawled your eyes out. Just then, a sturdy country lad approaches with his travelling equipage.

LOUISA   His what?

FIDDLE   It's a euphemism.

FANNY   It's a suitcase.

LOUISA   Oh no. I came from a village.

Pause.

Then this thing happened.

The whole village had to go.

Flat.

Pause.

FANNY/MRS COLE *(impatient)* The story

LOUISA The whole land was becoming one big farm

For miles and miles and it was an act of parliament.

And the village went quiet and rotted

And I couldn't get work.

I got hungry

Day after day after day after day

Like a knife

In the guts.

So then I got on the London road

But I never met a lad

FANNY/MRS COLE Oh dear...

LOUISA I met a girl

She had arms like twigs

And she never asked me nothing

But if I had some bread or a potato

FANNY/MRS COLE Where is this going?

LOUISA And then she took me where she lived, dead place,

And I went in through the door

And there were three dead people

All curled upon the floor

And two of them were children

And one was the mother

And they had straw in their mouths

Which they'd been eating.

And I left. Got to London, got fucked, got paid for it.

They took the land but they left the bodies.

Pause.

FANNY My readers do not want the sordid stink of suffering, they want a hard-on.

FANNY/MRS COLE Still, salvation is at hand.

Look. Here is a customer.

She pulls back the sheet. They are lewdly exposed. **DINGLE** *scurries to serve in the scene.*

It is Mr Norbert.

Originally a gentleman of great fortune and constitution, both now sadly impaired by his over violent pursuit of the vices of the town.

SONG: "WOULD YE HAVE A YOUNG VIRGIN"

DO YE FANCY A WIDOW WELL KNOWN IN A MAN?
WITH A FRONT OF ASSURANCE COME BOLDLY ON,
LET HER REST NOT AN HOUR, BUT BRISKLY, BRISKLY,
PUT HER IN MIND HOW HER TIME STEALS ON;

RATTLE AND PRATTLE ALTHOUGH SHE FROWN,
ROWSE HER, AND TOWSE HER FROM MORN TO NOON,
SHEW HER SOME HOUR Y'ARE ABLE TO GRAPPLE,
THEN GET BUT HER WRITINGS, AND ALL'S YOUR OWN.

DO YE FANCY A PUNK OF A HUMOUR FREE,
THAT'S KEPT BY A FUMBLER OF QUALITY,
YOU MUST RAIL AT HER KEEPER, AND TELL HER, TELL HER
PLEASURE'S BEST CHARM IS VARIETY.
SWEAR HER MUCH FAIRER THAN ALL THE TOWN,
TRY HER, AND PLY HER WHEN CULLY'S GONE,
DOG HER, AND JOG HER, AND MEET HER AND TREAT HER,
AND KISS WITH TWO GUINEA'S, AND ALL'S YOUR OWN.

WOULD YE HAVE A YOUNG VIRGIN OF FIFTEEN YEARS,
YOU MUST TICKLE HER FANCY WITH SWEETS AND DEARS,
EVER TOYING, AND PLAYING, AND SWEETLY, SWEETLY,
SING A LOVE SONNET, AND CHARM HER EARS:
WITTILY, PRETTILY TALK HER DOWN,
CHASE HER, AND PRAISE HER, IF FAIR OR BROWN,

SOOTH HER, AND SMOOTH HER, AND TEASE HER, AND PLEASE HER,
AND TOUCH BUT HER SMICKET, AND ALL'S YOUR OWN.

He has fallen into a taste for virgins.

Afternoon.

DINGLE/MR NORBERT Afternoon.

FANNY/MRS COLE Trade is very good at the moment, very good.

The wind has blown something my way, Mr Norbert. A country girl.

Blown all the way from Aberystwyth.

Intact.

(aside) He's like a dog drawn to a bitch.

Her name is Fanny.

The others move aside from the scene. **FANNY** *hovers.*

DINGLE/MR NORBERT How d'you do?

SWALLOW/FANNY Well, thank you, Mr Norbert.

DINGLE/MR NORBERT How old are you?

FANNY/MRS COLE She's fifteen.

DINGLE/MR NORBERT And new to town?

FANNY/MRS COLE Pristine.

SWALLOW/FANNY I am learning to make hats and live with this kindly milliner.

Hats are fascinating and come in different sizes.

DINGLE/MR NORBERT Gosh.

FANNY/MRS COLE *(aside)* He will pay a dazzling sum.

The others begin to prepare the next scene. Bringing a candle and a jar with a blood-soaked sponge in it.

It would be a sin not to make market of such fellows. They make good dupes, we make a good fifty quid.

The night is fixed!

The candles are lit.

DINGLE *and* **SWALLOW** *are alone. He approaches.*

SWALLOW/FANNY No.

DINGLE/MR NORBERT Yes.

SWALLOW/FANNY No.

DINGLE/MR NORBERT Yes.

SWALLOW/FANNY No.

She gives him a push. He overbalances.

DINGLE/MR NORBERT My dear.

SWALLOW/FANNY Go away.

DINGLE/FANNY Don't be afraid.

Come to me, my sweet, untouched goods!

He gets close to her. Begins to unbutton.

SWALLOW/FANNY I shall be ruined, I shall.

Lord, what are you about?

This is bitter usage!

Help! Help!

DINGLE/MR NORBERT Innocent, innocent.

SWALLOW/FANNY What is that?

DINGLE/MR NORBERT What?

SWALLOW/FANNY That.

She points to his crotch.

Do not bring it near me, for I do not like the look of it.

He laughs. Climbs on top of her.

I am afraid it will kill me!

(aside) His machine is of one of those sizes that slips in and out without being much minded.

Lord! I was never so used in all my born days!

DINGLE/MR NORBERT Just a little wider.

SWALLOW/FANNY 'Oh, I shall die, You have killed me' et cetera,

DINGLE/MR NORBERT Oh, rapture! Oh, my little unimpaired cargo.

SWALLOW/FANNY Little by little I suffered myself to be prevailed upon,

Spreading my thighs insensibly and yielding him liberty of access so that he got a little within me.

DINGLE/MR NORBERT Ah!

SWALLOW/FANNY But I worked the female screw so nicely *(she twists)* that I created an artificial difficulty of entrance which made him win me inch by inch with the most laborious of struggles.

DINGLE/MR NORBERT *(struggling)* Inch by inch.

SWALLOW/FANNY At length, with might and main, he winds his way completely home and gives my virginity, as he thought it, the final coup de grâce.

DINGLE *makes appropriate grunting noises.*

He was like a cock clapping its wings over his downtrod mistress.

DINGLE *makes a triumphant sound something like a cock crowing.*

Whilst I lay acting the deep wounded, undone and no longer maid. *(To him)* Alas! I am ruined!

DINGLE/MR NORBERT There, there. Do not cry.

I must get a little sleep.

He falls asleep.

She gets up quietly and fetches the jar with the sponge.

SWALLOW/FANNY A tumbler full of blood.

A sponge that requires no more than gently reaching the hand to it and when it is taken out and squeezed between the thighs, it yields plenty enough to save a girl's honour.

She squeezes the blood over her thighs, her shift, she rubs it in a bit.

And I will make thee beds of roses

And a thousand fragrant posies.

Mr Norbert. Mr Norbert.

Blood.

DINGLE/MR NORBERT My jewel.

SWALLOW/FANNY Blood. Blood. Blood.

FANNY One blood is quite enough.

She continues writing.

LOUISA *(to* SWALLOW*)* You're getting it everywhere.

SWALLOW *continues to dab herself.*

DINGLE She is merely working with industry, Miss Louisa.

LOUISA Industry?

DINGLE Hard work. Honest hard work.

There are laws.

Whatsoever thou sowest.

I worked hard.

First I owned one sixteenth...

They speak the next two lines simultaneously.

LOUISA ...of a ship and then I owned half.

DINGLE ...of a ship and then I owned half.

Pause.

And then it sunk.

But, you see, I'd been caught in a net,

Tangled in it.

FANNY How does one spell 'bifurcate'?

DINGLE Adrift on a sea of intemperateness.

Tempted.

Then those same pure laws

That elevate man to his highest condition

They cast me down.

A storm of retribution.

You see my point.

LOUISA I got headache.

FANNY 'Globule'?

DINGLE Things eating away at my pure condition, crumbling soft timber, like a pox.

FANNY 'Hirsute'? Or shall I put plain old 'hairy'?

LOUISA Headache. *(To* **DINGLE***)* That's you.

DINGLE Crumbling, Miss Louisa.

LOUISA Lice-shag!

He moves away.

SWALLOW Have we finished?

FANNY I've not yet reached my optimum target of encounters.

SWALLOW What do I do now?

FANNY You stay with Mr Norbert and become his mistress.

SWALLOW And we will sit upon the rocks

And see the shepherds feed their flocks.

FIDDLE Did you ever know a Mr Norbert?

FANNY Who?

FIDDLE A Mr Norbert?

FANNY I did it in the dark a lot. It's hard remembering things in the dark. The Norberts from the Dashwoods from the Drybutters.

FIDDLE Oh.

SWALLOW I stayed with Mr Norbert.

Sometimes he would sit me stark naked on a carpet by a good fire and contemplate me for an hour, kissing me in every part. His touches were exquisitely wanton and luxuriously diffused as if by his invention he meant to make up for his capital deficiency.

FIDDLE I think I would like a man with a capital deficiency.

FANNY Who asked you?

FIDDLE Luxuriously diffused sounds rather nice. That's all. Better than all the pumping and thrusting.

FANNY Pumping and thrusting?

FIDDLE Yes.

She demonstrates.

Like that.

FANNY Arch Jade!

FIDDLE I think I would still prefer one of Mr Norbert's propensities.

FANNY A fondler.

FIDDLE Yes.

FANNY Well, hard luck, 'cos he dies.

DINGLE Amen.

FIDDLE Poor Mr Norbert. I wish I'd never said anything.

FANNY Flinging young Fanny here back onto the open market.

SWALLOW No condition of life is more subject to revolutions than that of a woman of pleasure.

Music. Stage clears as **SPARK** *enters.*

SPARK Revolution?

FANNY Kind benefactor.

SPARK Can the winds of change have blown as far as this foul corner?

FANNY Happily, no. That sort of thing is best left to abroad.

SPARK I am of a revolutionary outlook.

I've read Rousseau.

It is my belief that things are only good or bad in reference to pleasure or pain. That we call good is apt to increase pleasure in us. Ergo, to fuck is good.

FANNY How nicely put.

SPARK I have cast off the abrasive shackles of conformity.

FANNY Talking of abrasive shackles...

SPARK And live a libertine's life.

FANNY I need a little help.

A few moments of your time. We were just about to evoke the scenario of the rod.

SPARK Indeed.

FANNY There are some poor few under the tyranny of this cruel taste.

SPARK Perverts.

FANNY Some require it to quicken those flagging, shrivelly parts that rise to life only by virtue of a sharp thwack and others just fancy it. Dreadful.

SPARK What does it entail?

FANNY A rod.

Someone throws her a rod.

And some rope.

And some rope.

I keep the rod.

The recipient of the lash has their hands tied.

She signals. Someone comes and ties his hands.

And that is how the whole beastly and offensive business begins.

SPARK I see.

It cannot be enjoyed.

FANNY Some miserable wretches achieve a vestige of titillation, yes.

SPARK Impossible.

FANNY You are a man of the new age.

SPARK I am.

FANNY Then allow me. An experiment. Scientific.

She gives him a slight tap.

Anything?

SPARK Nothing.

She hits him again.

FANNY That did not hurt?

SPARK No.

FANNY Or that?

SPARK Nor gave me any pleasure whatsoever.

FANNY Tut tut.

As little bothered as a lobster by a flea bite.

I'll try a little harder.

She hits him.

SPARK A little discomfort but I assure you not the slightest arousal.

FANNY Fancy that.

Hits him hard.

SPARK Ow!

FANNY A result!

SPARK But no gratification.

FANNY P'haps due to a wilful disposition?

SPARK The experiment is clearly defunct. Untie me.

FANNY So soon? I 'xpect you was a handful at school.

SPARK Untie me. Bulk-mongerer.

FANNY Don't turn nasty. This is scientific, remember.

She hits him again.

SPARK Ow!

She pokes him with the rod. Knocks him to the floor. Climbs over him.

FANNY I smelt desire. I'm sure I did.

Procured at the hands of pain.

SPARK Liar.

FANNY I saw it I did.

A stirring.

Your little wren peeping its head out of the grass and shuddering into life as each lash skimmed the surface of your cliffs so chubby and white cheeked.

Ergo, what a turn-up.

She laughs.

SPARK I'm giving you one more chance. These ropes. Loosen them.

FANNY There is talk of revolution.

Oh yes.

Right here.

This rod, for instance, is sharp.

SPARK Festering baggage.

FANNY How foolish to misprize an armed woman and in your position.

Now you will hear my business.

As you know I have been engaged in artistic endeavours aimed at pleasuring a grateful readership.

My memoirs.

Well, my book is my book.

I have written it and I will put my name to it and take all the profits and be excessive rich.

Oh, people will scrape low for me, very low.

I shall attend literary salons and chaff about being a tart and I shall wear impertinent headgear and be constantly accompanied by three singing birds and I will have diamond heels and eat only the icing off of cakes and if I wake at night a brawny chap shall sing to me and there will be a hundred silver bells strung about my person and my cats shall be scented and I shall swig grog and daily masturbate before a thundering warm fire in my boudoir and you can piss off, pimp.

SPARK I still have your debts.

FANNY Trifling things soon dealt with.

SPARK Stinking whore.

FANNY Arse breath.

Find someone else to pick out your splinters.

Untie his feet.

Someone does so.

SPARK This is not the end.

FANNY Farewell. It's been a pleasure.

SPARK I'll see you in the stocks.

He goes.

FANNY A triumph!

I almost remembered something then.

A good sign.

FIDDLE How fortuitous.

FANNY Exactly. I'd have two pasts then. A real one and one to make money with.

Life takes such strange turns.

I feel quite elevated.

Pause.

She kisses her book and starts to sing in celebration.
FIDDLE *and* **LOUISA** *join in at length.*

SONG: "A VINDICATION OF TOP KNOTS AND COMMODES"

THOSE SILLY OLD FOPS THAT KISS BUT LIKE POPES,
AND CALL US STREET WALKERS AND FAIRIES,
GO FUMBLE OLD JOAN AND LET US ALONE,

AND NEVER COME NEAR OUR CANARIES.
WE'LL WEAR OUR BREATS BARE WITHOUT FEAR, WITHOUT
    CARE,
AND SHOW OFF OUR CHARMS TO THE PEOPLE. BUT AS I'M A
    WHORE, ONE WORD FROM YOU MORE,
I'LL KICK YOUR ARSE OVER BOW'S STEEPLE.

LOUISA *gives a gasp.*

LOUISA Christ!

She doubles up.

Christ!

FANNY What's the matter?

LOUISA I'm shaking. Look, shaking.

FANNY We've got to get on.

LOUISA *gives a short cry.*

LOUISA Can't stop.

DINGLE She's shaking.

LOUISA Cold and bloody shivering.

DINGLE And white.

FANNY You took something.

LOUISA Powder. Tasted of metal.

FANNY The cure'll probably finish for you.

LOUISA I paid for 'em,

FANNY You was ripped off.

LOUISA I've got a pain.

DINGLE She's sick.

LOUISA Get lost.

Sings.

THOSE SILLY OLD FOPS THAT KISS BUT LIKE POPES...
CAN'T SING.

Pause.

I owe 'em my sovereign.

FANNY Life is expensive.

Next is the story of Louisa and the good-natured idiot, Dick.

LOUISA I'm resting!

FANNY He is a seller of nosegays.

She tosses **DINGLE** *something he can use as a nosegay.*

He is strong as a horse though in somewhat ragged a plight and smelly.

LOUISA I'm not doing it.

FANNY A wayward fancy seizes Louisa.

LOUISA No, I said.

FANNY She winks at him. Asks him upstairs.

DINGLE/NOSEGAY SELLER She has a strange longing to be satisfied.

LOUISA No!

DINGLE/NOSEGAY SELLER She encourages him with her eyes.

FANNY He drops his baskets.

FANNY repeats bits of DINGLE's litany as she makes notes. She almost overlaps with him.

DINGLE/NOSEGAY SELLER Through his rags she discovers his thighs and then the genuine sensitive plant...

FANNY Sensitive plant...

DINGLE/NOSEGAY SELLER ...which, instead of shrinking from her touch, joys to meet it and swells and vegetates...

FANNY Vegetates...

DINGLE/NOSEGAY SELLER ...under it. The waistband unskewers to reveal the whole of Dick's standard of distinction in full pride and display and such a one...

FANNY Such a one!

DINGLE/NOSEGAY SELLER ...it was positively of so...so tremendous a size it...

FANNY So tremendous a size...

DINGLE/NOSEGAY SELLER ...it astonished and surpassed all expectation, its enormous head...

FANNY Enormous head...

DINGLE/NOSEGAY SELLER ...seemed not unlike a common sheep's heart.

FANNY A common sheep's heart!

DINGLE/NOSEGAY SELLER You may even have trolled dice securely on the broad back of the body of it...

FANNY And the length too was prodigious. Oh, Louisa's appetite was up.

LOUISA It wasn't!

DINGLE/NOSEGAY SELLER The springs of his organ were wound to an extreme pitch.

LOUISA I'm going to puke.

DINGLE/NOSEGAY SELLER She took the fall she loved...onto the bed.

He faithfully directed his label of manhood, his battering point... And his joys became furious...

FANNY Furious...

DINGLE/NOSEGAY SELLER ...his eyes shoot fire. His teeth churning, his face glowing, his frame raging...

He has approached **LOUISA** *and has grabbed her.*

LOUISA Let go!

FANNY Raging...

DINGLE/NOSEGAY SELLER Ungovernable, butting, goring, wild, overdriven,

FANNY Goring...and what?

DINGLE/NOSEGAY SELLER He ploughs up the tender furrow.

LOUISA Let go of me!

FANNY *whispers as many of these words as she can follow.*

DINGLE/NOSEGAY SELLER Nothing can stop, blind rage, piercing rending tearing splitting...

LOUISA *breaks free.*

LOUISA LET GO!

DINGLE/NOSEGAY SELLER Splitting...

LOUISA My turn.

DINGLE *(quieter)* Splitting...

LOUISA Now I shall tell you about mine.

My favourite bits.

My choice bits which give me hot nights.

DINGLE *shies away.*

My mouth, my small tongue ever ready,
My little woman in a boat.

She won't bite,
But can be ravishingly touched by me or others.
Such exquisite vibrations, such shudderings.
Such delicious delirium and drenching pleasures, such riotous times and sweet excesses.
All mine.
Mine mine mine.

Yes.

Oh yes!

FANNY That is all very well, Louisa, but not for my book.
Gentlemen are more interested in their own bits.

LOUISA *continues to attack* DINGLE.

LOUISA Come on then. Come on.

Now.

Let's see your label of manhood now.

Let's see the lank and flapping thing!

Let's have more insupportable delight.

He backs away a bit; puts his hand on his crotch.

No?

Pity.

I want a drink!

She sits down heavily. She seems ill.

DINGLE Miss Louisa.

Pause.

Miss Louisa.

He approaches.

You're poxed.

LOUISA I want a drink.

DINGLE Poxed. Poxed a hundred times over.

FANNY Pay no heed to Doctor Dingle.

LOUISA Come closer and I'll spew.

DINGLE I came here for you.

LOUISA What?

DINGLE For you. To rescue you.

LOUISA Me?

DINGLE From drowning. Sinking.

> I have submitted myself to foul and licentious practices for your sake, Miss Louisa, for your sake only.

LOUISA Nutter.

DINGLE I am your salvation.

FANNY Enough of your pulpit pimpery, we are writing a novel.

DINGLE Profane things are practiced here in our very streets which have made this city a second Sodom!

LOUISA Get away.

DINGLE You must renounce your way of life and come with me.

> This is my card. I won't use force.

> It's all voluntary.

He holds out a card. She does not take it.

FANNY Dingle, you ponce. You've taken a puritannical turn. It's highly repugnant.

DINGLE I am in disguise.

> I belong to an organisation.

> We call ourselves 'night walkers'.

> We walk out and about at night, saving souls.

> That's when I spotted you.

> We are out to end the horrid debauchery of the age.

LOUISA Fucking help.

DINGLE It starts with the harlot. That's you.

> You tempt us. You turn us off course.

> We neglect things. We lose money. Then we steal to pay for your filthy services. This leads to quarrellings and

fightings, clamours of 'murder', breaking of windows and other tumultuous riots, routs and uproars. Property is lost. The state is enervated. The pox spreads to wives and families, soldiers and sailors and they are effeminated. Sailors are effeminated and ships sink. Ships sink. They sink. You sunk my ship.

LOUISA I never bleedin' touched it.

DINGLE Ships are lost. Trade is lost. Colonies are lost. Wars are lost. The whole country is lost. Lost.

FANNY I fear you have a case of rumpled premises, Mr Dingle.

DINGLE I will be heard, Miss Fanny. I will be. You must think of your future life, Louisa.

LOUISA I want to get through this one.

DINGLE Repent.

LOUISA I'll eat now and pray later.

DINGLE Turn your back on evil.

FANNY It's only sticking a penis up her and twiddling it about a bit.

DINGLE Once a whore always a whore.

LOUISA You've dabbled. I've seen you. Round here. Before. Maybe even done you.

DINGLE I paid. I paid. My Louisa sunk.

LOUISA Go home.

Pause.

DINGLE You're dying.

Pause.

Dying.

LOUISA No.

DINGLE Dying.

LOUISA What do you know?

Pause.

I'm fine.

DINGLE You're burning now.

LOUISA Fine.

DINGLE A death fever.

LOUISA No.

FANNY No.

DINGLE A hell fever.

FANNY No!

DINGLE Dying.

Pause.

I know a place. A hospital. A pure place.

FANNY All this morbidity! And with our end in sight. I suggest you bugger off, Dingle, and leave us to our art.

DINGLE Death and damnation, Miss Louisa!

Pause.

I pity you.

I had hoped to save you but see I am too late.

Fanny Hill. I do not know strong enough terms with which to express my repugnance for your opus.

Goodbye.

FANNY He has a certain dexterity of phrase, I'll give him that.

He begins to leave.

LOUISA Wait!

Pause.

Wait.

She gets up.

FANNY Louisa?

SWALLOW Louisa?

LOUISA *looks at them and follows* **DINGLE** *out.*

FANNY *(shouts)* Louisa!

FIDDLE They've gone.

FANNY *(calls after them)* I'm not paying you!

Pause.

(to **SWALLOW***)* I still have you left, my little bird. You will help me finish my story.

FIDDLE She's got blood on her face.

FANNY Spit on your hanky, rosebud, and wipe your face.

FIDDLE It's on her dress too. Blood.

SWALLOW A gown made of the finest wool

Which from our pretty lambs we pull.

Nothing happens. **FIDDLE** *offers* **SWALLOW** *her hanky.*
SWALLOW *takes it. Begins to wipe her face.*

FIDDLE *(to* **FANNY***)* Did you have a daughter, ever?

FANNY I might have. I might not.

FIDDLE I just wondered.

SWALLOW Wipe, wipe, wipe.

FANNY Let us have a lively tune.

FIDDLE *complies.*

We've had a glut of pleasure already, but why stop there?

We will resume our history.

It's time young Fanny met a rich old gentleman.

SWALLOW Come live with me and be my love.

FANNY A rational pleasurist. Much too wise to be ashamed of the joys of humanity and with a fat bank balance.

SWALLOW Wipe, wipe my face. It's all over my face.

FANNY Come along. You've been such a good girl to Fanny thus far, it would be a shame to let her down at the very denouement. I shall give you a pretty setting. The park. Plenty of foliage plus ample opportunities for hasty concealment. What do you say?

SWALLOW I lied about the wiping.

FANNY Never mind that.

SWALLOW It wasn't a sore but it ran down his leg.

Sometimes he stuck it in my mouth where I sat but I wouldn't swallow, I spat it out later.

Sometimes he let me touch his books.

His room was warmer than the rest.

He always had a fire and a plate of apples.

I liked his voice when he read.

I always wiped up after.

But then I got bigger and I couldn't wipe that up, no.

FANNY You meet the old gentleman in the park.

SWALLOW Then he told me to go.

He wouldn't look me in my eyes.

No more words.

No more shepherds.

I left.

I walked for four days.

FANNY The old gentleman makes you sole executrix of his will in an indecent short time.

SWALLOW I couldn't go home like it.

So I went to a new place.

I knocked on the door of the church-warden but he would not open it.

So I sat on his step.

In the morning they made me leave the parish because I had a belly on me and they did not want it born where they would have to upkeep it.

They were poor and hardworking they said and I must go elsewhere.

So I went in the fields.

In the snow.

Later there was blood in the snow and I moaned in it and staggered a mad dance in it and the baby came.

FANNY An indecent short time.

SWALLOW I carried her all day and she was screaming.

Sometimes I sat in the snow.

I did not know what to do.

In my mind I called her Annie.

I did not know what to do.

So I tied her in my hanky and came to a river

Then I dropped her in the river and she did float a little and sink fast.

She was light but she sank fast.

FANNY A short time.

SWALLOW That is murder.

FIDDLE Murder...

SWALLOW I did not know how to keep her.

FANNY What does the old gentleman ask of you?

SWALLOW To bite the ends off his gloves.

FANNY Lovely. You've got an imagination.

SWALLOW There was a girl hung at Iveschester.

She was strangled by having the stool taken from under her.

She killed her baby. It took them six weeks to find her.

FANNY Silk or kid, the gloves?

SWALLOW They always find you. Annie will float into a port and they'll come and get me.

FANNY Not yet.

SWALLOW They they'll hang me.

FANNY You've got too much imagination.

SWALLOW I want to ask you. I've been thinking.

Put me in your book.

FANNY So close. So close to the end.

SWALLOW I did not know how to keep her, write that.

FANNY We can finish before dark, if we hurry.

SWALLOW People will hate me otherwise.

They'll hate me for ever and they won't know.

Write me in your book so they won't hate me.

Don't write soft things. Write me.

FANNY That's not how the world goes.

SWALLOW How does it go?

FANNY That sort of thing won't sell.

It would be like reading a report.

SWALLOW They strangled her first so as to stop her talking out. Saying things. True things.

FANNY Who'd want to read a thing like that?

SWALLOW They choke you off at the neck.

Put about me in your book.

It's not the dying.

I might lie in a grave wanting to tell.

Twisting about.

Put me in your book, please.

Pause.

Just a page.

Pause.

FANNY No.

SWALLOW Then your book will be a lie

She cried so much I tore out some of my hair.

I left that in the snow too.

Goodbye.

FANNY Where are you going?

SWALLOW Which way?

FANNY No one will look for you here. Not today.

SWALLOW The found her in six weeks.

She goes.

FANNY Fuck!

Pause.

This book needs one last fuck.

Pause.

I'll have to do it alone.

That's life for you.

She prepares herself.

I intend this last fuck to be a very happy fuck. Proving that a whorish life is a rewarding life.

And if the sober amongst us object I have this to say: A fart upon you.

Music please.

That last old rich gent inadvisedly runs to a window on an alarum of fire and stands there naked and exposed to the fatal impressions of the damp night air. Which proves fatal.

A funereal note.

I was then in the full bloom of my youth, and being his sole heiress and executrix, rolling in it.

Anyway, one night I drove to this inn and I called to this coachman to fetch me down, he had on a great cape and a hat which flapped about his chops, and as he approached the thing flew off, owing to a freak gust, and there he stood. 'My life! My soul! My Charles!'

DINGLE *and* **SPARK** *walk on still in shadow.*

My dearest Fanny, says he, can it be you?

And then we snogged.

Unutterable delight! Sweet confusion!

We hired a private room immediately.

SPARK *walks in.*

SPARK This is a love story.

Your customers won't want this slop, Fanny.

They want their appetites fed. They want meat.

FANNY I'm getting to the meat.

I was soon laid in bed, and Charles, after a short, prelusive dalliance, lifted up my linen and his own and laid his bare chest next to my bosom, beating now with the tenderest alarms.

DINGLE *comes in.*

DINGLE Filth! Pure and unadulterated.

FANNY I loved Charles with all my heart.

SPARK They don't want romance, they want flesh.

FANNY The powers of solid pleasure thickened upon me.

DINGLE It's dirt.

FANNY Charles, my love.

SPARK Where is the dirt?

FANNY I was now in touch at once with the instrument of pleasure and the great seal of love, I lay overwhelmed, absorbed, lost in an abyss of joy and dying of nothing but immoderate delight.

FIDDLE Oh, well done, Miss Fanny!

DINGLE Vice!

SPARK Still a trifle fleshless.

FANNY I feel the delicious velvet tip! Oh, my pen drops from me in ecstasy!

FIDDLE Oh my!

FANNY I had now taken in love's true arrow and soon began the driving tumult on his side and the responsive heaves on mine.

FIDDLE Goodness!

FANNY Sparks of love fire ran all over, blazing in every vein, every pore of me. Soon our joys grew too mighty for utterance! And oh!

FIDDLE Oh!

FANNY Now!

FIDDLE Now!

FANNY I felt it to the heart of me, now!

> **FANNY** *gives a final gasp.*

DINGLE Sex!

SPARK Romance!

FANNY My book has mixed them both, sirs, into the greatest of joys!

FIDDLE Bravo, Miss Fanny!

FANNY Thank you.

> Charles and Fanny are soon married and live happy and wealthy ever after.
>
> Thus I have satisfied both the square and the scurrilous amongst you.
>
> I shall be rich!

> *She kisses her book.*

FIDDLE I thought that last passage quite...diverting.

> **FANNY** *kisses it again.*

SPARK Is that it? The book?

FANNY It is. My sweet salvation.

DINGLE Diverting, she called it.

FANNY Entertaining, enlightening, pleasuring.

SPARK I've come for it.

> **FANNY** *laughs.*

FANNY I told you. It's mine.

DINGLE Diverting.

SPARK The book.

FANNY No.

DINGLE *(indicating* FIDDLE*)* If it should fall into the hands of the likes of her. An innocent wench. Where would it lead?

FIDDLE Where?

SPARK I'm afraid you have little choice in the matter.

DINGLE Reading has spread to all sorts. You can't see a woman but she has a new-fangled novel tucked into her purse.

SPARK New laws.

FANNY New laws.

SPARK The contagation of licentious publications are fatal to the unguarded minds of the youth of both sexes.

DINGLE Not to mention servants and women.

SPARK We're on state business.

FANNY What business?

DINGLE There are worse fates than illiteracy!

SPARK This book is an insult upon religion and good manners.

DINGLE Nakedness and books are dangerous.

SPARK If you're going to show vice, it must disgust. Not please.

FANNY A book can please as nature pleases!

SPARK While art must imitate nature it is necessary to distinguish those parts of nature which are proper for imitation.

DINGLE Your book is about nothing but copulation!

FANNY Some books are about nothing but ships and there are no objections.

DINGLE This book is merely an account of the flesh trade.

FANNY The whole world does a trade in that, Mr Dingle. Nothing's free or haven't you noticed?

SPARK This book is an inflammatory text and fit for the fire.

FANNY The fire!

SPARK In the wrong hands it could be the beginning of a serious decline.

DINGLE Good novels are about decent married people raising a family!

SPARK So. Give it to me.

FANNY No!

DINGLE The book is perilous!

FANNY To a fool. But are fools worth the least attention?

SPARK Hand it over.

FANNY No! I will not let you have it. Never! No!

SPARK Then I shall fetch a bishop.

And a justice. The penalties are most severe.

Pause.

FANNY I am ruined.

She still holds her book.

DINGLE *(calls)* Louisa!

LOUISA *enters. She is dressed in grey, tight, constricting clothes, her hair is scraped back. She carries a large iron box and some keys. She does not look about her.*

FANNY Louisa! It's me. Fanny.

Pause.

We cannot let them do this.

LOUISA *unlocks the big iron box. She holds out her hand for the manuscript.*

Louisa?

DINGLE   The obscene knows no bounds. It flies into the remotest corners of the earth, penetrating into the obscurest habitations and corrupting the simplest hearts.

LOUISA   There's nothing you can do.

She takes the manuscript from FANNY *and places it in the box.*

DINGLE   This is our strong box. Treble-locked. I belong to this organisation. We have collected nearly one thousand lewd prints, four hundred and seventeen books, French and English, and well over sixteen hundred bawdy common songs.

It's a beginning.

Well, I've work to do. I cannot stay.

May you see the light, Miss Fanny.

Good day.

He exits.

SPARK   Perhaps this has shown you your place in the world.

FANNY   Hypocritical ponce! My only satisfaction is in knowing that your profit too is scuppered!

SPARK   Oh no. No.

He laughs.

You labour under a misapprehension, Miss Fanny. I am starting a whole shining new enterprise. Yes, books must be spanking clean and free from the sordid infiltrations of desire but there will still be a market for such carnalities.

And where there is a market there is a way.

And where there is a prohibition there is a profit.

And I intend to make it, under the counter so to speak.

FANNY   You could never write a book.

SPARK No. But then I won't need to. I'll be dealing in pictures, pure sleaze, no storyline.

Times change and one must move with the times.

So, I'll say my goodbyes.

The pleasure's been all mine.

FANNY May your globular appendages be ulcerated.

He salutes. Exits.

Louisa! Louisa! Don't let them do it!

Slip it back to me! On the quiet.

LOUISA I can't.

FANNY Why?

LOUISA I'm a Magdalen girl now.

FANNY Magdalen?

LOUISA Like a church. Like a hospital.

Up at five. Sweat out our badness in laundries.

There's loads of us. Then we've work to do.

I collect things. Songs.

FANNY You weren't dying.

LOUISA Wasn't I?

FANNY No.

LOUISA I would have done. Soon enough.

FANNY Delicious delirium.

LOUISA We're forbidden to speak of the past.

We're in bed by nine. Lights out ten past.

Hands on top of the covers.

FANNY Lord!

LOUISA Things are changing, Fanny. Stiff collar times are coming. We take baths in our petticoats.

FANNY What for?

LOUISA I dunno.

DINGLE *(calls from offstage)* Louisa!

LOUISA I've got to go.

She starts to close the box, then remembers.

I nearly forgot. I've a song to put in the box.

She opens the box and sings into it.

Sings.

MY LADY HAS A THING MOST RARE
ROUND ABOUT IT GROWS MUCH HAIR
SHE TAKES DELIGHT WITH IT IN BED
AND OFTEN STROKES ITS HAIRY HEAD.

FANNY What is it?

LOUISA A lap dog.

They both laugh raucously.

DINGLE *(calls)* Louisa!

LOUISA I must go.

She shuts up the box. Composes herself.

Goodbye, Fanny.

She walks out briskly.

FANNY She's gone.

FIDDLE Gone for good.

FANNY All for nothing. Everything for nothing.

Pause.

FIDDLE No one ever asked me anything.
About myself, I mean.

She comes forward.

I was the daughter of a parson. All I wanted to do was to play music but of course there was nowhere for girls to study. My father died and my brother inherited everything. So I...

FANNY Oh, shut up.

Pause.

FIDDLE Is Fanny your real name?

FANNY No, it was a joke.

FIDDLE I don't get it.

FANNY Never mind.

FIDDLE What was your name?

FANNY I don't know. Something beginning with an E. Or a P. Or a T.

FIDDLE You never remember anything.

FANNY No. I seem to have forgot myself.

FIDDLE Oh dear.

FANNY Sometimes I have this dream. God says, 'Fanny, you may have one wish,' so I ask for some holes. Then whoosh just like that all these holes appear all over me, small at first but big enough to stick a finger in. I'm delighted. What a time I'll have with these, I think. I have tripled in value and tripled again. And then my mouth opens wider and wider and all the holes get bigger still and bigger till finally all the holes join up at the edges until I'm just one big hole. Big enough for God or a giant reader to fuck and then I disappear.

Pause.

I disappear.

FIDDLE What a funny dream.

Pause.

Shall I play you something?

What's your favourite?

FANNY *opens her mouth but can't reply.*

Don't remember?

Pause.

Then I shall play something for myself.

Something...diverting.

Pause.

If a book like that should be read by an innocent wench...
like me...where would it lead?

Where?

She smiles.

She plays and sings a version of **"MY LADY HAS A THING
MOST RARE"**. *She laughs. She stretches luxuriously,
she slides her hands between her legs. She looks out.
She smiles.*

Where?

Lights down.

End

PROPS/SOUND EFFECTS

PART ONE

PROPS
Knife (p4)
Coin (p7)
Bottle (p8)
Violin (p10)
Gin bottle (p22)
Purse (p26)
A letter (p37)
A sock (p37)
Cane (p44)

COSTUME
Voltaire – dressed circa eighteenth century (p1)
Swallow – coat (p29)
Louisa – dressed as a boy (p36)
Lighting
Lights up (p1)
Lights focus on this [bed] (p25)
Lights focus on Swallow (p29)
Lights down (p45)

SOUND/EFFECTS
A mist (p1)
Fiddle – from now on she plays to accompany moments, scenes (p11)
Intro on the violin (p24)
Sounds of rustling (p25)
Flourish on her violin (p35)

PART TWO

PROPS
Pillow (p48)
Card (p49)
A large sheet (p49)
A candle and a jar with a blood-soaked sponge in it (p54)
A rod (p61)
Rope (p61)
A nosegay (p66)

A card (p70)
Hanky (p73)
A large iron box and some keys (p82)
Manuscript (p82)

COSTUME
Louisa – dressed in grey, tight, constricting clothes, her hair is
scraped back (p82)
Lighting
Lights down (p87)

SOUND/EFFECTS
The violin plays (p46)
Long note from the violin (p47)
An instrumental note (p48)
A funereal note (p78)
She plays and sings a version of "MY LADY HAS A THING
MOST RARE" (p87)

THIS IS NOT THE END

Visit samuelfrench.co.uk and discover the best theatre bookshop on the internet

A vast range of plays
Acting and theatre books
Gifts